DATE DUE

NOV 2 8 2012
NOV 3 0 2015

Geese

Geese, Ganders, and Goslings

Lorijo Metz

PowerKiDS press™

New York

On the Farm

To Suzanne Slade, may her quill never run dry

Published in 2011 by The Rosen Publishing Group, Inc.
29 East 21st Street, New York, NY 10010

First Edition

Editor: Amelie von Zumbusch
Book Design: Greg Tucker
Photo Researcher: Jessica Gerweck

Photo Credits: Cover, pp. 4, 5, 6, 8, 9, 10, 11 (bottom), 12, 13, 14, 15, 16, 17, 18, 19, 20, 21 Shutterstock.com; p. 7 © www.iStockphoto.com/Hanne Melbye-Hansen; p. 11 (top) Joel Sartore/Getty Images; p. 22 Monty Rakusen/Getty Images.

Library of Congress Cataloging-in-Publication Data

Metz, Lorijo.
  Geese : geese, ganders, and goslings / Lorijo Metz. — 1st ed.
      p. cm. — (On the farm)
  Includes index.
  ISBN 978-1-4488-0692-8 (library binding) — ISBN 978-1-4488-1345-2 (pbk.) —
  ISBN 978-1-4488-1346-9 (6-pack)
  1. Geese—Juvenile literature. I. Title. II. Series: Metz, Lorijo. On the farm.
  SF505.3.M48 2011
  636.5'98—dc22
                                                                  2010006837

Manufactured in the United States of America

CPSIA Compliance Information: Batch #WS10PK: For Further Information contact Rosen Publishing, New York, New York at 1-800-237-9932

Contents

Waterfowl

Geese are part of the waterfowl family. Waterfowl are birds that swim and live near water. While the goose that laid the golden egg is only a fairy tale, real geese supply people with many useful things. For about 3,000 years, people have raised geese for meat, eggs, and feathers. Long ago people used feathers, called quills, made from goose feathers.

Farm geese, such as this one, are good swimmers. However, they spend less time in the water than wild geese do.

Farm Facts

Baby geese are goslings. Father geese are ganders. Mother geese do not have a special name. They are just called geese.

4

Today, many people in the United States, including members of 4-H Clubs, raise geese to show at county and state fairs. **Economically,** however, goose farming remains most important in Asia and central Europe.

Geese can live in places with many different kinds of weather. For this reason, they are raised on farms around the world.

What Do Geese Look Like?

Geese have long necks and fat bodies covered with feathers. They have flat beaks, called bills. A goose's knees are hidden beneath its stomach feathers. The part of a goose that looks like a backward knee is really part of the goose's foot! As other birds do, geese walk on their toes. The rest of their foot never touches the ground.

Here, you can see this goose's long neck and large body. Geese on farms tend to have larger bodies than wild geese do.

In most **species** of birds, males are more colorful than females. However, in almost every **breed** of geese, the males and females look the same. Pilgrim geese are the only exception. Male Pilgrim geese are creamy white, while the females are olive gray.

Many of the geese raised on farms have white feathers, as the geese in this group do.

Swimming and Flying

Geese have four toes. They have one short toe in back and three long toes in front. Their front toes are **webbed.** Their webbing makes goose feet look like paddles. It also makes them good for swimming. Geese swim by pushing their webbed feet backward and downward through the water.

Their webbed feet help geese, such as these two, move quickly and smoothly through the water.

Wild geese are known for the V shape that a group of them makes when flying. **Domesticated** geese, on the other hand, do not spend much time in the air. Many of them do not fly well. Some are too heavy to fly at all. Others have had their wings **trimmed** so that they will not fly away.

Even when they are not swimming, geese like to spend time in and around water. These geese are wading in a river.

These wild Canada geese are flying in the V shape that wild geese often form when traveling.

Wild Geese and Domesticated Geese

Domesticated geese look much like wild geese. However, they tend to be larger. Many domesticated geese are raised for meat. They were **bred** to be big to have more meat.

There are two main groups of domesticated geese. Geese from Europe are **descended** from the wild greylag goose. Greylag geese are one of the largest kinds of wild geese in Europe. Geese from Asia descend from the wild swan goose.

There are many kinds of wild geese. Canada geese, such as those here, are the most common wild geese in North America.

These breeds have longer, swanlike necks. They also have lumps where their beaks meet their heads. They are often smaller than European geese. While wild greylag geese and swan geese are generally gray, some domesticated geese are almost all white.

This is a greylag goose. In the past, the numbers of greylag geese fell because the marshes they lived in were being built on. Today, the geese are making a comeback.

This goose is an African goose. African geese are descended from swan geese. In spite of their name, they come from China.

Breeds of Domesticated Geese

In the United States, Toulouse geese are one of the breeds most often raised for meat. People also raise these geese for **exhibition**. Toulouse geese raised for exhibition can weigh up to 25 pounds (11 kg). Their bodies can be so large that they seem to drag on the ground.

This bird is a Toulouse goose. Toulouse geese were first raised near the French city of Toulouse.

While most geese are raised for meat, you might be surprised to learn that people also use geese as guard animals. Geese will honk loudly at strangers. They have good eyesight, so they can see

predators from far away. Though they are the smallest domesticated breed, Chinese geese make excellent guard geese. They are also the best egg layers.

Most of the Pomeranian geese in North America are saddlebacks. This means they have a patch of dark feathers on their backs, as these geese do.

These are Embden geese. Embden geese are white, with orange bills. They are the tallest breed of goose.

Fuzzy Goslings

Mother geese lay eggs. After about 30 days, the eggs begin to **hatch**. The goslings inside tap on the eggshells with their beaks until the eggs break open.

On some farms, goslings spend their days following their mothers around. On other farms, goslings are not raised with their mothers. Instead, they live with other goslings. Farmers use **heat lamps** to keep these goslings

This small gosling is about a week old. Goslings grow quickly.

warm. They also supply the goslings with a dry place to stay when it rains. All goslings are born with down. These fuzzy feathers are different from the feathers adult geese have. Down does not keep goslings dry.

Though they need a dry, warm place to get away from bad weather, it is also good for goslings to spend time outside.

What Do Geese Eat?

Geese eat mostly plants. Farmers feed geese grains, such as corn. When they are outside, they geese find their own food. They eat several kinds of grasses but can be picky eaters. Farmers sometimes use geese to control weeds in crops such as cotton and strawberries. The geese eat the weeds but leave the crops alone. These geese are called

All animals need water. Along with food, farmers must give geese water to drink.

Farm Facts

Geese sometimes swallow little stones. The stones go to their gizzards. There, they help break down the birds' food.

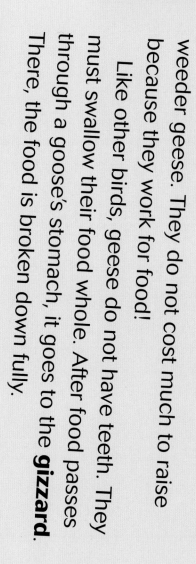

weeder geese. They do not cost much to raise because they work for food!

Like other birds, geese do not have teeth. They must swallow their food whole. After food passes through a goose's stomach, it goes to the **gizzard**. There, the food is broken down fully.

Chinese geese, such as the birds shown here, are often used as weeder geese. This is because the Chinese goose is an active breed.

Goose Flocks

Geese live in groups, called flocks. They are smart birds and remember things well. They form close bonds with other geese. Wild geese stay with the same partner, or mate, for life. On farms, geese do not mate for life. However, they are close to the other members of their flocks.

Goose flocks, such as this one, come in many sizes. They can have a handful of geese or thousands of geese.

Geese make loud noises called honks. No one knows exactly why geese honk, though. Some people believe they honk to say hello. Geese may also honk to warn of danger and to give **encouragement** to other geese.

This goose is honking. Goose honks are very loud. Because they are so noisy, geese are not generally raised in crowded neighborhoods.

Eating Geese

Goose meat is darker than chicken meat. It has a richer taste, too. In the United States, goose meat is most often eaten on holidays. In northern Europe, people eat goose meat all year round. Goose eggs are common in dishes from China and other parts of Asia.

Predators, such as owls, foxes, and raccoons, also like to eat

This goose has been roasted. Roasted goose is one of the most common ways that goose is served.

Farm Facts

Foie gras, or fattened goose liver, is highly prized by the French. It has a rich, buttery taste.

geese and goose eggs. Farmers use fences to keep predators away from geese. They use dogs to guard geese, too. Geese also fight back when they are in danger. They stick out their necks, hiss, and charge at their enemies.

This angry goose is hissing. If a goose hisses at you, stay away from it. If you go closer, the goose may think that it needs to defend itself by charging at you.

Goose Down and More

Most geese that are raised for meat and eggs can also supply down and feathers. On an adult goose, down is a soft, fluffy **layer** of feathers found under a goose's longer outer feathers. It is used to stuff blankets, pillows, and winter coats. Goose down is soft

Geese are smart animals with their own personalities. Many people find that they make good pets.

and light. It is also very good at keeping in heat.

People have been raising geese for thousands of years. In that time, we have found so many uses for these birds. Geese are here to stay!

Glossary

bred (BRED) To have brought a male and a female animal together so they will have babies.

breed (BREED) A group of animals that look alike and have the same relatives.

descended (dih-SEN-did) Born of a certain family or group.

domesticated (duh-MES-tih-kayt-id) Having to do with animals people picked to breed together.

economically (eh-kuh-NAH-mih-kuh-lee) Having to do with business.

encouragement (in-KUR-ij-ment) Hope given to another.

exhibition (ek-suh-BIH-shun) A public show.

gizzard (GIH-zurd) Part of an animal's body that helps break down food.

hatch (HACH) To come out of an egg.

heat lamps (HEET LAMPS) Lamps that supply heat.

layer (LAY-er) One thickness of something.

predators (PREH-duh-terz) Animals that kill other animals for food.

species (SPEE-sheez) One kind of living thing. All people are one species.

trimmed (TRIMD) Had parts cut off.

webbed (WEBD) Having skin between the toes, as ducks, frogs, and other animals that swim do.

Index

A
air, 9

B
breed(s), 7, 11–13

E
egg(s), 4, 13–14, 20–22
Europe, 5, 10, 20
exhibition, 12

F
farming, 5
feathers, 4, 6, 15, 22

G
gizzard, 17

H
heat lamps, 14

L
layer, 22

M
meat, 4, 10, 12, 20, 22

P
pens, 4

P
predators, 13, 20–21

Q
quills, 4

S
species, 7

T
toes, 6, 8

W
water, 4, 8
wings, 9

Web Sites

Due to the changing nature of Internet links, PowerKids Press has developed an online list of Web sites related to the subject of this book. This site is updated regularly. Please use this link to access the list:

www.powerkidslinks.com/otf/geese/